D1303594

1 9 8 6
The Year
I Was Born

Compiled by Sally Tagholm

Illustrated by Michael Evans

FANTAIL

in association with Signpost Books

FANTAIL PUBLISHING, AN IMPRINT OF PUFFIN ENTERPRISES
Published by the Penguin Group
Penguin Books Ltd, 27 Wrights Lane, London W8 5TZ, England
Penguin Books USA Inc., 375 Hudson Street, New York, NY 10014, USA
Penguin Books Australia Ltd., Ringwood, Victoria, Australia
Penguin Books Canada Ltd, 10 Alcorn Avenue, Toronto, Ontario, Canada
M4V 3B2
Penguin Books (NZ) Ltd, 182–190 Wairau Road, Auckland 10, New Zealand
Penguin Books Ltd., Registered Offices: Harmondsworth, Middlesex,
England
Published by Penguin Books in association with Signpost Books

First published 1992
10 9 8 7 6 5 4 3 2 1

Based on an original idea by Sally Wood
Conceived, designed and produced by Signpost Books Ltd, 1992
Copyright in this format © 1992 Signpost Books Ltd.,
25 Eden Drive, Headington, Oxford OX3 0AB
England

Illustrations copyright © 1992 Michael Evans
Text copyright © 1992 Sally Tagholm

Editor: Dorothy Wood
Art Director: Treld Bicknell
Paste up: Naomi Games

ISBN 1 874785 06 6 Hardback edition
ISBN 0140 90369 0 Paperback edition

All rights reserved

Colour separations by Fotographics, Ltd.
Printed and bound in Belgium by Proost Book Production through
Landmark Production Consultants, Ltd.

Typeset by DP Photosetting, Aylesbury, Bucks

All rights reserved. Without limiting the rights under copyright reserved
above, no part of this publication may be reproduced, stored in or
introduced into a retrieval system, or transmitted, in any form or by any
means (electronic, mechanical, photocopying, recording or otherwise),
without the prior written permission of both the copyright owner and
the above publisher of this book.

MY FAMILY

ME

Name: Josie
Date of birth: 1986
Time of birth:
Place of birth: hospitil
Weight at birth:
Colour of eyes: Drown
Colour of hair (if any): Drown
Distinguishing marks:

MUM

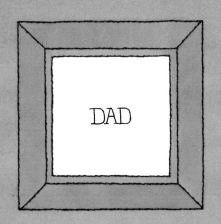

DAD

SISTER/BROTHER

SISTER/BROTHER

January

Wednesday *January 1*	Spain and Portugal join the European Economic Community, bringing the total number of members to 12. Israel gets a new shekel, it equals 1000 old ones, and is the size of a shirt button.
Thursday *January 2*	The Queen grants 38 new Royal Warrants to tradesmen, including suppliers of pea harvesting equipment, plastic bags, forklift trucks and smoked salmon.
Friday *January 3*	The Model Engineering Exhibition opens at the Wembley Conference Centre in London. On show is a scale model of the *Mary Rose* made out of 500,000 matchsticks.
Saturday *January 4*	The Lord Mayor holds a Fancy Dress Party for children at the Mansion House in London.
	Snow in the Midlands
Sunday *January 5*	Birdwatch UK 1986, Britain's biggest ever birdwatch, is organised by the RSPB and the Wildfowl Trust. More than 160 different species are spotted by about 25,000 twitchers at 150 sites.
Monday *January 6*	Last chance from now until the middle of the month to see Halley's Comet from Britain before it disappears behind the sun, re-emerging towards the end of February.
Tuesday *January 7*	Blizzards block roads and close schools in Wales. New 12p stamps for Scotland, Wales and Northern Ireland go on sale.
Wednesday *January 8*	A new £2 coin is issued by the Royal Mint to commemorate the Commonwealth Games to be held in Edinburgh this summer.
Thursday *January 9*	NASA announces that the *Voyager 2* spacecraft has found a sixth moon in orbit around Uranus. Ron Grant (42) finishes a 281.575km run across the Simpson Desert in Australia in just over $3\frac{1}{2}$ days.
Friday *January 10*	Torrential rain and floods. Sheep drown in Kent and Hampshire. The Common Market Commission launches European Road Safety Year. New Moon
Saturday *January 11*	British expedition, led by Robert Swan, reaches the South Pole at 11.53am GMT after 14 months and 1,420.747km.
Sunday *January 12*	Motorway near Rosenheim in Bavaria is closed for 7hrs after a lorry turns over and spills 24.384 tonnes of noodles.
Monday *January 13*	St Hilary's Day: traditionally the coldest day of the year. Snow blocks the Mont Blanc tunnel between France and Italy and has to be blown up with dynamite.

January

Named after the Roman god Janus, who had two faces and could look backwards and forwards at the same time; also known as 'frosty-month', 'after-yule', 'first-month' and 'snow-month'.

THE MOTOR CAR
A CENTENARY CELEBRATION

1886: Patent for the first car with a petrol-driven internal combustion engine issued to Karl Benz

1906: Rolls Royce make the first Silver Ghost

1908: The 'Tin Lizzie' is born: the first Model-T Ford costs $900

1913: The first Morris Oxford is produced

1925: White lines are painted on roads for the first time

1935: Sir Malcolm Campbell sets new world land speed record in Bluebird of 301.337mph

1959: The Mini car is born

1983: A new law makes wearing a seat belt compulsory for drivers and front seat passengers

1986: European Road Safety Year

January 14: Four new stamps are issued to celebrate Industry Year

17 PENCE · INDUSTRY YEAR/1986

22 PENCE · INDUSTRY YEAR/1986

31 PENCE · INDUSTRY/YEAR 1986

34 PENCE · INDUSTRY YEAR 1986

Grapevine ▲

140 MILLION YEAR OLD TORTOISE FOUND IN CHINESE COAL MINE

Good.Egg ◖

LEANING TOWER OF PISA ONLY MOVES 0.48mm IN LAST YEAR

Chatterbox ▣

SOUTH POLE EXPEDITION'S SUPPORT SHIP SINKS IN ICE

Newsreel ◍

POLICE AT HEATHROW TO GET GUNS

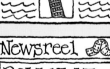

Tuesday *January 14*	Worst gales of the winter sweep Scotland at 144.81km/h. The island of Colonsay off the west coast is cut off from the mainland for the eighth day running.
Wednesday *January 15*	Walt Disney open The Living Seas at the Epcot Center in Florida. It is 8.23m deep, and is as big as two football pitches with more than 4000 species of marine life.
Thursday *January 16*	The Duke of Edinburgh launches Industry Year. A mallard duck with a broken wing is rescued from the road between Midhurst and Chichester by a bus driver and taken to the bird hospital at Eartham.
Friday *January 17*	More than 5000 skiers are stranded in the Austrian Alps when 274.32cm of snow falls in less than 36hrs.
Saturday *January 18*	Captain Scott reached the South Pole in 1912. Sampson, a golden retriever, is rescued 12 days after falling over a cliff in Devon onto a ledge.
Sunday *January 19*	Storms and gales sweep Britain: roads are blocked by fallen trees. A gust of 120.675km/h is recorded in London.
Monday *January 20*	First national holiday in USA to honour the late Martin Luther King, who fought for the rights of black Americans. Channel Tunnel launching ceremony in Lille, France.
Tuesday *January 21*	Concorde's 10th birthday: the special anniversary flight from London to New York takes just 3hrs 22mins. 4.064 tonnes of Cheddar cheese is stolen from a trailer at Evercreech in Somerset.
Wednesday *January 22*	A 9.08kg sturgeon, caught off Beachy Head, is taken to Buckingham Palace as a gift for the Queen.
Thursday *January 23*	Measles epidemic in Northamptonshire: there have been 174 new cases reported in the last 3 weeks. A snowman 7m high is spotted at Val d'Isère in France.
Friday *January 24*	The US spacecraft *Voyager 2*, launched on August 20, 1977, flies within 81,542.5km of the planet Uranus. It flew past Jupiter in 1979 and Saturn in 1981.
Saturday *January 25*	Burns Night celebrates the anniversary of the famous Scots poet's birth in 1759. Special Young Ornithologists' Club Garden Bird Watch between 9–10am.

Bird Watch

Sunday *January 26*	A mouse-eared bat is found in Sussex: it is at least 13yrs old and is thought to be the only one left in Britain. Full Moon
Monday *January 27*	The Ecology Party is re-named the Green Party. The European Figure and Ice Dance Championships begin in Copenhagen.
Tuesday *January 28*	The US space shuttle *Challenger* explodes 74secs after lift-off from Cape Canaveral, Florida.
Wednesday *January 29*	National Bat Year is launched. The Bishops of Tewkesbury and Taunton are consecrated at Gloucester Cathedral by the Archbishop of Canterbury, Dr Runcie.
Thursday *January 30*	LLANFAIRPWLLGWYNGYLLGOGERYCHWYRNDROBWLL-LLANTYSILIOGOGOGOCH, the railway station in Anglesey with the longest name in the world, is sold by BR for more than £150,000.
Friday *January 31*	The pirate station Radio Caroline is blown off the air when her ship breaks anchor in gale force winds in the North Sea.

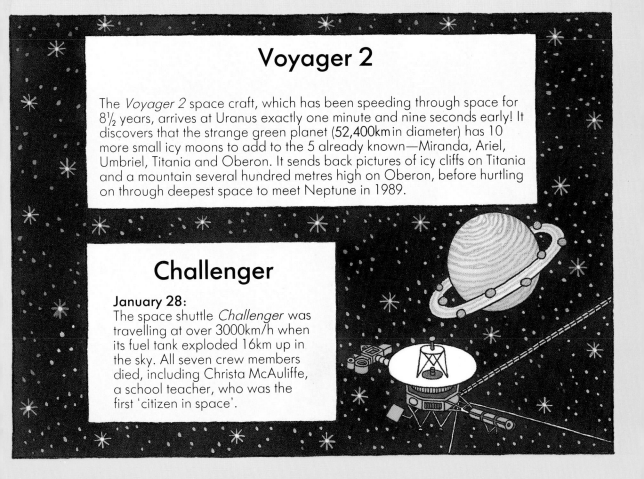

Voyager 2

The *Voyager 2* space craft, which has been speeding through space for 8½ years, arrives at Uranus exactly one minute and nine seconds early! It discovers that the strange green planet (52,400km in diameter) has 10 more small icy moons to add to the 5 already known—Miranda, Ariel, Umbriel, Titania and Oberon. It sends back pictures of icy cliffs on Titania and a mountain several hundred metres high on Oberon, before hurtling on through deepest space to meet Neptune in 1989.

Challenger

January 28:
The space shuttle *Challenger* was travelling at over 3000km/h when its fuel tank exploded 16km up in the sky. All seven crew members died, including Christa McAuliffe, a school teacher, who was the first 'citizen in space'.

February

Saturday *February 1*	Storms bring snow and rain to Europe: the lagoon in Venice rises 1.52m above sea level.
Sunday *February 2*	Beginning of Jolablot, part of the old Norse winter festival of Yule, when animals were sacrificed to encourage the return of the sun. 8 rare white-winged Wood Duck, bred at the Wildfowl Trust, leave Heathrow for India, where they will go to special breeding centres.
Monday *February 3*	State of emergency in SE France after violent blizzards. Cyclone Winifred batters Queensland, Australia, and ruins about a third of the banana crop.
Tuesday *February 4*	The royal train with the Queen on board breaks down 8 times between King's Lynn and London, arriving 46mins late at Liverpool Street Station!
Wednesday *February 5*	Henry Weston, who started running round the world on April 1, 1984 in London, to raise money for the World Wildlife Fund, sets off from San Francisco. He will run 25,744km through 28 countries.
Thursday *February 6*	Snow covers the country: Snake Pass in Derbyshire is closed. Only Heathrow airport stays open thanks to special crystals that are scattered on the runways to prevent them from freezing.
Friday *February 7*	First day of Cruft's Dog Show at Earls Court, London: 11,830 competitors take part in the 3-day event.
Saturday *February 8*	Archaeologists at Saqqara in Egypt discover the 3000 year old tomb of Maya, treasurer to the Boy King Tutankhamun. The *Sheffield Morning Telegraph* appears for the last time after 130 years.
Sunday *February 9*	Start of Chinese Year of the Tiger. A 3 year old Airedale terrier called Ginger Xmas Carol wins the Best In Show title at Cruft's. New Moon
Monday *February 10*	Palm trees at Lodmoor Country Park in Weymouth, Dorset, wear electrically-heated jackets to protect them from the cold.
Tuesday *February 11*	Pancake Day. Department of Health warns of a Whooping Cough epidemic: there have been nearly 4670 new cases since the beginning of the year.
Wednesday *February 12*	Beginning of Lent. The Channel Tunnel Treaty is signed in the Chapter House of Canterbury Cathedral.
Thursday *February 13*	Trial of the Pyx at Goldsmith's Hall tests samples of coins produced by the Royal Mint.

February

The Roman month of purification. It has also been known as 'sprout kale', 'rain-month', 'month of cakes' and 'month of ravaging wolves'.

Chinese Year of the Tiger

According to legend, the Buddha summoned all the animals in the world to him one New Year, and promised them all a reward. Only twelve obeyed and he gave them each a year: the Rat arrived first so he got the first year! The order of the 12-year cycle is always the same: Rat, Buffalo, Tiger, Cat, Dragon, Snake, Horse, Goat, Monkey, Cockerel, Dog and Pig.

   Tigers are very daring and they fight for what they believe is right. They can be great rebels and they like taking risks. But, on the whole, they are very lucky! They are also sensitive and generous. Tigers get on well with Horses, Dragons and Dogs but NOT with Snakes, Monkeys or Buffaloes! Famous Tigers include Emily Bronte, Beethoven, Louis XIV, Karl Marx, Marilyn Monroe and, of course, Queen Elizabeth II.

   The Chinese Year of the Buffalo ends on February 8. Buffaloes are quiet and patient, but are often *very* intelligent and can make good leaders. Famous Buffaloes include Richard the Lionheart, Napoleon and Charlie Chaplin.

In the Footsteps of Scott

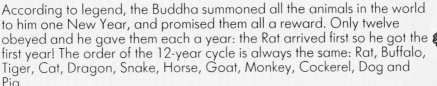

Robert Swan (28), Roger Mear (35) and Gareth Wood (33) set out from their Base Camp at Cape Evans on Nov 2 last year— exactly the same day that Captain Scott left for the South Pole in 1911. They trek 1420km across the snow and ice, retracing Scott's last journey. They pull all their food and equipment themselves on sledges that weigh more than 136kg. They cover about 7.5km each day and arrive at the South Pole 6 days earlier than Captain Scott. Captain Scott buried secret stores of food in the snow on his way to the South Pole in 1911–12. They were for the journey back which, very sadly, he didn't quite make. One of them was found this month at Butter Point on McMurdo Sound after warmer weather made the snow banks shift. In it are tins of cocoa, jam, sardines, egg powder, candles and matches. They are all at least 74 years old!

February 18:   Four stamps issued to celebrate Halley's Comet

Friday *February 14*	St Valentine's Day. It's freezing. Whitbread Round the World Race gets ready to leave Auckland, NZ, to sail for Cape Horn.
Saturday *February 15*	A hot air balloon reaches 6165m in Texas and sets a new world record. Barry McGuigan retains his featherweight title in Dublin.
Sunday *February 16*	The Queen and the Duke of Edinburgh leave Heathrow for a state visit to Nepal followed by a trip to New Zealand and Australia.
Monday *February 17*	Princess Anne has tea at the Savoy Hotel, London, with the 77th Blackburn St James' Brownies pack. Brownies all over the country raised £179,000 for the Save the Children Fund selling cups of tea.
Tuesday *February 18*	Child of Achievement Awards in London. Cricketer Mike Gatting gets his nose broken in the opening one-day international match in Kingston, Jamaica.
Wednesday *February 19*	The Soviet Union launches a new orbital space station. It's called *Mir*, which means peace.
Thursday *February 20*	A perfect black tulip has been grown in Holland after 25 years of trying. Halley's Comet comes out from behind the sun.
Friday *February 21*	Mr Shigechiyo Izumi (120) dies in Japan: according to the *Guinness Book of Records* he was the oldest man in the world.
Saturday *February 22*	European rocket Ariane is launched from the French Space Centre at Kourou in French Guinea.
Sunday *February 23*	It's so cold that the sea freezes in Southampton, Rhyl and Christchurch. Full Moon
Monday *February 24*	Good news for golden eagles, peregrine falcons and ptarmigans: the RSPB buys 2146.5 hectares of mountain in Scotland.
Tuesday *February 25*	New decorations for the roof of the south transept of York Minster, which was badly damaged by fire in 1984, are unveiled.
Wednesday *February 26*	The Eleven Towns Race in Holland. It's an ice race along 201.125km of canals and has only been held 13 times in 100 yrs.
Thursday *February 27*	Fire destroys nearly 40,000 pine trees near Poole Harbour in Dorset. Helicopters drop water bombs on the flames.
Friday *February 28*	The Dutch coaster *Stern* is stranded on Great Yarmouth beach after being blown ashore by gale force winds.

UK Fact File 1986

United Nations Year of Peace   Year of the Bat

European Road Safety Year   Industry Year

Total area of the United Kingdom   244,100 sq kms

Average population per sq km   233

Population of UK   56,763,000

Births   755,000

Deaths   Marriages
660,700   393,900

Members of Parliament   650 (27 are women)

Members of the European   81
Parliament (British)
                                     Head of State
Prime Minister   Queen Elizabeth II
Margaret Hilda Thatcher

                                     Archbishop of Canterbury
                                     Robert Alexander
Poet Laureate   Kennedy Runcie
Edward (Ted) Hughes

                                     Astronomer Royal
                                     Prof F Graham Smith

Members of European Community: Belgium, Denmark,
France, Federal Republic of Germany, Greece, Irish Republic,
Italy, Luxembourg, Netherlands, United Kingdom, Spain, Portugal

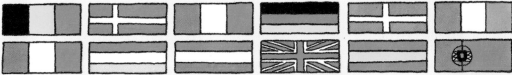

Most popular girls' name*   Elizabeth

Most popular boys' name*   James

* according to *The Times* newspaper

March

Saturday *March 1*	St David's Day. The British and European Worm Charming Festival in Devon is postponed because the ground is frozen.
Sunday *March 2*	Age Concern launches Cold Crisis Campaign: they send out 1000 kits including a fuel voucher, packets of soup and a body warmer.
Monday *March 3*	The teachers' pay dispute is settled after more than a year. Teachers will get a pay rise of 6.9% rising to 8.5% at the end of the month.
Tuesday *March 4*	*Today* newspaper is launched by Eddie Shah. High heels are banned from National Trust properties in Wales: visitors will be provided with plastic slippers. Soviet spacecraft *Vega 1* flies within 8029km of Halley's Comet.
Wednesday *March 5*	RAF Spitfire PM 631, which took part in the Battle of Britain, flies over the City of London and past the Houses of Parliament to celebrate the 50th anniversary of its maiden flight.
Thursday *March 6*	Bob Geldof launches Sport Aid in London to raise money for famine relief in Africa.
Friday *March 7*	The 193.08km of waterways that make up the Norfolk Broads are to become a National Park.
Saturday *March 8*	Japan's 1.22m long *Suisei* spacecraft says hello to Halley's Comet from a distance of 151,000km.
Sunday *March 9*	Mothering Sunday. Soviet *Vega 2* flies within 8030km of Halley's Comet. Teams of 3 take part in a sponsored 6-legged race from King's College, Cambridge to Grantchester to raise money for the Save the Children Fund.
Monday *March 10*	Commonwealth Day. Prince Edward is 22. Young Citizens' Award Ceremony at the Mansion House. New Moon
Tuesday *March 11*	Japan's *Sakigake* spacecraft gets within 6,990,000km of the nucleus of Halley's Comet, which is shrinking by about 50.8 tonnes a second according to the scientists.
Wednesday *March 12*	British Rail gives 66.825 hectares of land to the British Wildlife Appeal including Harbury Spoilbank, Warks: an important butterfly habitat and home to the rare bee orchid.
Thursday *March 13*	The Walls' Pocket Money Monitor shows that the average weekly pocket money for 5–16 year olds is up 7% to £1.17. Soviet Union launches two cosmonauts on a mission to the new *Mir* space station.

March

Named after Mars, the Roman God of War. It has also been known as 'rough-month', 'lengthening-month', 'boisterous-month' and 'windy-month'.

The Dirty Snowball

Halley's Comet travels in a huge orbit round the Sun and won't be back until you're 76! The Chinese first spotted it in 250BC and the Normans watched it before the Battle of Hastings in 1066. They recorded it in the Bayeux Tapestry. The *Giotto* space craft, launched last July and named after the Italian artist who painted Halley's Comet as the Star of Bethlehem, has the closest encounter ever with the comet this month. It sends back more than 2000 images of the comet showing that it's rather like a large dirty snowball, measuring about 9.4m × 6.2m with a nucleus 'the darkest dark you can imagine'.

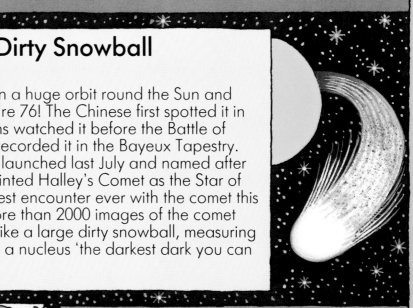

The American Wonder Lemon

The American Wonder Lemon (Citrus limon 'Ponderosa') comes from a tree that was planted in 1980 from a cutting grown at the Botanical Gardens in Birmingham. Although it is so enormous, the rind is very thick and it's not very juicy. It makes a special appearance on 'Blue Peter' but, when it is cut up and squeezed, it only produces about one eggcupful of juice!

Town Crier
USSR NAMES SEVEN ASTEROIDS AFTER SPACE SHUTTLE CHALLENGER CREW

Daily Sensation
HERD OF DUGONGS SIGHTED IN THE GULF

The Owl
DIVERS DISCOVER THE LOST CAVE OF CHEDDAR

News Today
FIRE SWEEPS THROUGH THE SOUTH WING OF HAMPTON COURT PALACE

Friday *March 14*	European spacecraft *Giotto* travelling at 68km per second gets nearest to Halley's Comet at 539.015km. Photographs sent back show that the core is 15km long and that it is one of the darkest bodies of the solar system.
Saturday *March 15*	262 Shire Horses take part in the National Show at the East of England Showground, Peterborough.
Sunday *March 16*	The largest lemon in Britain has been grown in Pershore, Worcs. It weighs 2.128kg and is nearly 61cm in circumference. It's known as an American Wonder Lemon.
Monday *March 17*	St Patrick's Day: the Queen Mother presents shamrocks (in short supply this year because of bad weather) to the Irish Guards at Chelsea Barracks, London.
Tuesday *March 18*	Budget Day: income tax is cut by 1p to 29p in the £. The Showmen's Guild announces that goldfish in plastic bags will be banned from the annual Sloe Fair at Chichester.
Wednesday *March 19*	Buckingham Palace announces the engagement of Prince Andrew and Sarah Ferguson. The engagement ring is a large oval ruby set in ten drop diamonds on a yellow and gold white band.
Thursday *March 20*	A plaque in memory of Percy Shaw, who invented cats' eyes (reflective road studs) in the 1930's, is unveiled at his birthplace in Boothtown, nr Halifax, Yorks.
Friday *March 21*	The spring equinox and the first day of spring. In danger: a family of rare Daubenton bats who live under a bridge in Rushton, Northants, that is threatened with demolition.
Saturday *March 22*	More than 100 competitors take part in the third British and European Worm Charming Championships in Devon: the winner coaxes 149 worms from 1 sq m of soil in 15mins.
Sunday *March 23*	Police stop a 183cm Cornish pasty being pushed from Callington, Cornwall, to Bristol for charity because it is a hazard to road safety.
Monday *March 24*	A hurricane hits southern England at 161km/h: roofs are ripped off and trees blown down. The Severn bridge is closed to all traffic for the first time ever.
Tuesday *March 25*	Lancelot, the Bewick's Swan, leaves the Wildfowl Trust at Slimbridge, Gloucs, after his 23rd winter there. He's off to his breeding grounds in the Arctic.

Wednesday *March 26*	The new *HMS Sheffield* is launched on the River Tyne: the old one was sunk in the Falklands War. Full Moon
Thursday *March 27*	Maundy Ceremony at Chichester Cathedral: 60 men and 60 women each receive 60 pence in special silver coins. Domesday 900 Exhibition opens in Winchester, where the Domesday Book was compiled.
Friday *March 28*	Good Friday. 80 drivers leave Belfast City Hall at 9am at the start of the 2413.5km Ireland Motor Rally.
Saturday *March 29*	Cambridge wins the 132nd University Boat Race. They beat Oxford for the first time since 1975 by 7 lengths in 17mins 58secs.
Sunday *March 30*	Easter Sunday. Summer time begins at 1am when the clocks go forward by one hour. St Augustine volcano erupts in Alaska, sending ash and gas 2743.2m into the air.
Monday *March 31*	Bank Holiday. Goodbye to Greater London Council and the metropolitan counties of Greater Manchester, Merseyside, Tyne and Wear, West Midlands, South and West Yorkshire.

Family 1986

On average, each member of Family 1986 drinks 2.35 litres of milk each week and eats 118gm of cheese, 1.05kg of meat, 146gm of fish, 3.01 eggs, 297.4gm of fat and oil, 284.3gm of sugar, 3.32kg of fruit and vegetables and 1.5kg of cereals.

Weekly Shopping Bill For One

Milk and cream	103.85p
Cheese	33.91p
Meat	284.59p
Fish	50.41p
Eggs	20.24p
Fats and oils	36.15p
Sugar and preserves	17.57p
Fruit and vegetables	197.64p
Cereals	159.76p
Total	904.12p (£9.04)

(These figures are taken from the National Food Survey)

April

Tuesday *April 1*	April Fools Day. The new Terminal 4 building at Heathrow airport in London is opened today. The St Augustine volcano blocks out the sun in Alaska.
Wednesday *April 2*	Scientists in Moscow are planning a new space mission to Mars called Project Phobos.
Thursday *April 3*	The Domesday Book goes on display at the Public Records Office in London as part of its 900th anniversary celebrations. Two French sailors arrive in Miami, Florida, after crossing the Atlantic on a specially equipped sailboard in 24 days.
Friday *April 4*	10 Soviet spacemen start lying flat on their backs for a year, with their feet kept permanently at an angle of 5° above their heads, to find out what the effects of a VERY long space flight might be.
Saturday *April 5*	West Tip wins the Grand National at 15–2—ridden by Richard Dunwoody (22), the youngest jockey in the race.
Sunday *April 6*	A stagecoach travels from London to Rochester, Kent, to mark the 150th anniversary of Charles Dickens' journeys in 1836. It takes 5hrs.
Monday *April 7*	On display at Sledmere House, Bridlington, North Yorks: more than 2000 lead soldiers in a re-creation of the 'Delhi Durbar' when the new King George V was presented to India for the first time.
Tuesday *April 8*	A pop song called *The Queen's Birthday Song* is released to celebrate Her Majesty's 60th birthday on April 21. A new frigate *Coventry* is launched at Wallsend to replace the warship lost in the Falklands.
Wednesday *April 9*	Film star Clint Eastwood is elected Mayor of Carmel in California. New Moon
Thursday *April 10*	The first Shakespeare festival opens in China, including King Lear, Richard III and Othello.
Friday *April 11*	Tonight Halley's Comet's tail becomes very bright as it comes closest to Earth at only 68,000,000km.
Saturday *April 12*	Clowns' Convention at Bognor Regis, Sussex. The average daytime temperature in central London so far this month is only 5.7°C. Dormice are still hibernating because it's so chilly.
Sunday *April 13*	Barmouth Bridge across the Mawddach Estuary re-opens. Ship worms, nibbling away at the timber, caused £1,800,000 worth of damage.

April

The opening month—from the Latin 'aperire' which means to open. Also known as the time of budding, the cuckoo's May or the fool's May.

The Queen's Birthday Chart

Surname:	Windsor
Christian names:	Elizabeth Alexandra Mary
Time of Birth:	2.40am
Day of week:	Wednesday
Date:	April 21
Year:	1926
Place:	17 Bruton St, London W1
Mother:	Her Royal Highness the Duchess of York formerly Lady Elizabeth Angela Marguerita Bowes-Lyon
Father:	His Royal Highness Prince Albert Frederick Arthur George
Sign of Zodiac:	Taurus
Chinese Sign of the Zodiac:	Tiger
Lucky birthstone:	Diamond
Lucky flower:	Daisy

Chernobyl: April 26

An explosion at the Chernobyl nuclear power station in the Ukraine causes a devastating fire and the worst nuclear accident ever. A vast cloud of radio-active dust is blown all over Europe causing wide-spread contamination. Billions of litres of milk are thrown away, hundreds of thousands of sheep and cattle are put into quarantine and the long-term effects can only be guessed at.

April 28

The 1986 XIII Commonwealth Games £2 coin is the first commemorative coin ever to be issued in this country to celebrate a sporting event. On one side there is a thistle and a laurel wreath on top of St Andrew's Cross. On the other side there is the new portrait of the Queen by Raphael Maklouf.

In Danger: Ramosmania Heterophylla

RODRIGUEZ ISLAND
INDIAN OCEAN

THE ONLY CAFÉ MARRON TREE IS BEING EATEN BY BUGS & ANIMALS

APRIL 16 1986

TWO CUTTINGS FROM THE TREE ARE FLOWN TO LONDON

3PM APRIL 17 1986

THIS IS A GOOD CUTTING
THIS IS A POOR CUTTING

THEY ARRIVE AT THE PROPAGATING UNIT, KEW GARDENS

MIXTURE OF PEAT, GRIT & FERTILISER
CLEAR POLYTHENE

ONE CUTTING IS PLANTED IN PEAT & GRIT & KEPT AT 32°C

JUNE 20 1986

YIPPEE! IT'S GOT ROOTS

THE PROPAGATING UNIT NOTICE THAT SOME ROOTS ARE GROWING

JULY 4 1986

ACTIVE GROWTH STARTS TWO WEEKS LATER

Monday *April 14*	Sarah Ferguson's personal coat of arms is approved by the Garter King of Arms. It shows a bumblebee resting on a thistle. The motto is '*Ex Adversis Felicitas Crescit*' (from adversity happiness grows).
Tuesday *April 15*	Viv Richards, the West Indian Captain, hits the fastest Test century ever, in 56 balls, in the fifth Test against England in Antigua.
Wednesday *April 16*	Two rare cuttings travel by jet from the Indian Ocean to Kew Gardens, London: they're from a rare Café Marron tree on the island of Rodriguez. It's the only one left in the world and it's being eaten by mealy bugs.
Thursday *April 17*	The volcano at Mount St Helens in Washington State, USA, sends steam, gas and ash 7620m into the air. It last erupted in 1980.
Friday *April 18*	Snow blocks A6024 Holme Moss road in the Peak District. A blast at Cadbury's chocolate factory in Staffs causes £2,500,000 damage.
Saturday *April 19*	Great Britain v. France in the first women's Rugby International at Richmond Athletic Ground. The 24,384 tonne *HMS Hermes*, Britain's flagship in the Falklands conflict, is sold to India.
Sunday *April 20*	18,336 competitors take part in the 6th London Marathon. Japanese Toshihiko Seko (29) wins in 2hrs 10mins 2secs. The first woman across the finishing line is Grete Waitz (32) from Norway in 2hrs 24mins 54secs.
Monday *April 21*	Happy 60th birthday to the Queen! She receives 56,000 messages from all over the world.
Tuesday *April 22*	Jonathan Carter (9) becomes BR's Young Super Traveller of the Year after travelling 84,223km by train.
Wednesday *April 23*	St George's Day. An airship takes off from Leavesden airport near Watford. It's the first fare-paying airship flight since the Graf Zeppelin flew from South America to Germany in 1937.
Tuesday *April 24*	First day of Passover. Total eclipse of the Moon in the East from 11.04am until 2.22pm. Two men are sent to prison for 7 years in Hong Kong for stealing £40,000 worth of birds' nests from a medicine shop. Full Moon
Friday *April 25*	Crown Prince Makhosetive is crowned King of Swaziland: he is the 67th son of the late King Sobhuza.

Saturday *April 26*	The nuclear reactor at Chernobyl, in the Ukraine, blows up. It is *the worst* nuclear disaster ever. The effects are felt all over Europe.
Sunday *April 27*	Gerry Anderson (65) of Halberton nr Tiverton, Devon, becomes National Snuff Taking Champion after sniffing 50 samples without a cough or a sneeze.
Monday *April 28*	The Queen opens a new extension at the Battersea Dogs' Home in London.
Tuesday *April 29*	Happy 85th birthday to the Emperor of Japan! A family of badgers stops all work on a new housing estate nr Bracknell, Berks.
Wednesday *April 30*	Ban on the sale of mussels from the Wash. It's been one of the most thundery Aprils ever.

The Fox

WORLD'S WORST NUCLEAR REACTOR ACCIDENT IN USSR AT CHERNOBYL

Echo

BRITAIN'S FIRST SNAIL FARM OPENS IN SOMERSET

Daily Bell

RIP JACK THE SPOTTED TABBY BLUE PETER CAT

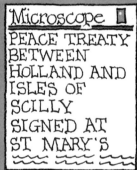

Microscope

PEACE TREATY BETWEEN HOLLAND AND ISLES OF SCILLY SIGNED AT ST MARY'S

The Happy Birthday Page!

The Royal Mint is 1100 years old
Ripon, Yorkshire, is 1100 years old
Domesday Book is 900 years old
Texas is 150 years old
The Mersey Tunnel is 100 years old
The Statue of Liberty is 100 years old
The motor car is 100 years old
The Salvation Army is 100 years old
Winnie the Pooh is 60 years old
BBC TV is 50 years old
The London A–Z Street Atlas is 50 years old
The Biro is 40 years old
The Wildfowl Trust is 40 years old
UNICEF is 40 years old
The National Youth Theatre is 30 years old
The Berlin Wall is 25 years old
The World Wildlife Fund is 25 years old
Concorde is 10 years old

May

Thursday May 1
May Day. The Sweeps' Procession is held in Rochester, Kent. The last time it was held was 1868, when sending children up chimneys was forbidden by law.

Friday May 2
An army remote control robot tries to blow up a suspicious parcel at Cardiff railway station: it turns out to be full of tea and curry powder.

Saturday May 3
The annual Tulip Time Parade in Spalding, Lincolnshire, features daffodils instead of tulips, which are late because of the cold weather. Belgium wins the 31st Eurovision Song Contest.

Sunday May 4
Carol (14) and Susan Firth (11) from Birmingham blow up the pier bandstand at Weymouth, Dorset. It was their prize for coming first in a special competition.

Monday May 5
Bank Holiday. More than 2,000 runners take part in the Belfast City Marathon: Marty Deane wins in 2hrs 16mins 5secs. Joe Johnson from Bradford beats Steve Davis by 18 frames to 12 to win the Embassy World Snooker Championships in Sheffield.

Tuesday May 6
Soviet cosmonauts Leonid Kizim and Vladimir Solovyov transfer from *Mir* to *Salyut-7* space station. It's the first time that this has ever been done.

Wednesday May 7
The Tortoise Sanctuary at Downham Market, Norfolk, advises owners to wake up tortoises still hibernating because of the cold weather.

Thursday May 8
A new rose is presented to the Queen to mark the official opening of the £30,000,000 National Garden Festival in Stoke-on-Trent. It's called 'Festival Rose' and is bright pink with cream and white stripes.

New Moon

Friday May 9
Swiss yacht *UBS Switzerland* wins the 43,500km Whitbread Round the World Race in 117days 14hrs 31mins, beating the '81–'82 record by 2days 16hrs and 2mins.

Saturday May 10
First day of Ramadan. Liverpool beats Everton 3–1 in the FA Cup Final at Wembley.

Sunday May 11
An official announcement is issued to all bird lovers in Britain: the ONLY pair of Golden Eagles nesting in England have hatched an egg in the Lake District. Wardens are keeping a 24-hour watch.

Monday May 12
St Pancras' Day. The House of Lords decides that it likes being on television after a trial run of 15 months.

May

Takes its name from Maia, the goddess of growth and increase, or from 'maiores', the Latin word for elders, who were honoured this month. The Anglo Saxons called it 'thrimilce' because cows could be milked three times a day now. An old Dutch name was 'bloumaand' which means blossoming month.

May 20:   PO issues 4 Europa Nature Conservation stamps

NATURE CONSERVATION
17P
SPECIES AT RISK
BARN OWL
(TYTO ALBA)

NATURE CONSERVATION
22P
SPECIES AT RISK
PINE MARTEN
(MARTES MARTES)

NATURE CONSERVATION
31P
SPECIES AT RISK
WILD CAT
(FELIS SILVESTRIS)

NATURE CONSERVATION
34P
SPECIES AT RISK
NATTERJACK TOAD
(BUFO CALAMITA)

Domesday Disc

The first proper written survey of England was carried out in 1086 for King William I. It listed all the land in the country, who it belonged to, and how much it was worth. Although it was called 'the description of England', it was known as the Domesday Book. You can see both volumes—Great Domesday and Little Domesday—at the Public Records Office in Chancery Lane, London.

Nine hundred years later, in 1986, a new hi-tech Domesday Disc is born—with a little help from 14,000 schools and other assorted groups like Guides, Scouts and Women's Institutes. For nearly two years they have been busy collecting all sorts of information on micro-computer about their particular areas. Little by little, they have pieced together a picture of modern-day Britain like a giant jigsaw made up of 85,000 photographs and 2,000,000 pages of facts and maps. The information gathered is the same as two complete sets of the *Encyclopaedia Brittanica* but it all fits on to two video discs!

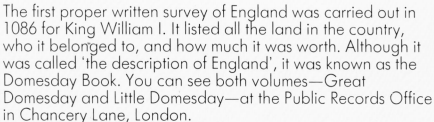
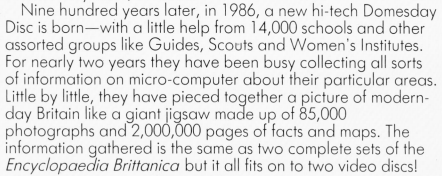

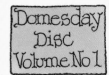

Domesday Disc Volume No 1

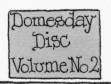

Domesday Disc Volume No 2

Tuesday *May 13*	Poor weather has wiped out over half of the bee-hives in Britain: English honey will be very scarce this year! 45 horses and riders gallop across Exmoor, Devon, on the Golden Horseshoe Long Distance Endurance Ride—80km yesterday and 80 more today!
Wednesday *May 14*	Simon Barnes (22), Andy Haynes (21) and Danny Aykroyd (23) set off in extra-light sports wheelchairs from John O'Groats to travel 1775km to Land's End. They should arrive at the end of June!
Thursday *May 15*	Top tennis stars in Rome to play in the Italian Open Championships present the Pope with a tennis racquet and a sports bag.
Friday *May 16*	Omar Khalifa lights an Olympic torch at a camp in the Sudan in Africa and sets off on a journey across three continents to launch next weekend's 'Race Against Time', which will raise money for famine relief. -2.1°C at Liphook, Hants
Saturday *May 17*	Appalling weather conditions in the Ten Tors trek across Dartmoor: only 300 of the 2400 competitors complete the course.
Sunday *May 18*	Happy 66th birthday to Pope John Paul! Ken Black (33) windsurfs round the Isle of Wight in just under 8hrs, knocks 1½hrs off the record and raises £3000 for the RNLI.
Monday *May 19*	Four hundred cats' eyes are stolen from a council store at Zeals, nr Warminster, Wiltshire.
Tuesday *May 20*	Building work starts on the new City Airport in London. 65th Chelsea Flower Show opens in London: 1986 Rose of the Year is 'Gentle Touch'. Violent thunderstorms, torrential rain and floods
Wednesday *May 21*	The last yacht in the Whitbread Round the World Race, the Danish *Sas Baia Viking*, crosses the finishing line at Gosport, Hants—12 days after the winner. Cooks at the Navy's Catering School at *HMS Raleigh* in Torpoint, Cornwall, secretly stir Prince Andrew and Sarah Ferguson's wedding cake.
Thursday *May 22*	National Bike Week is launched at the Royal Festival Hall in London. Full Moon
Friday *May 23*	The New China News Agency reports that a South China tiger, an almost extinct species, has been spotted in the province of Hunan.
Saturday *May 24*	Omar Khalifa takes the Olympic torch (May 16) to Buckingham Palace, at the beginning of Sport Aid's 'Race Against Time'.

Sunday *May 25*	30,000,000 people in 200 different cities take part in Sport Aid's 'Race Against Time'. 200,000 of them run in Hyde Park, London. The famous Lutine Bell, which tolls when ships sink at sea, is moved to the new Lloyd's building in the City of London.
Monday *May 26*	Bank Holiday. First 206km stage of the Milk Race, from Birmingham to Blackpool, is won by cyclist Steve Joughin, from the Isle of Man.
Tuesday *May 27*	300 canoeists in 285 boats link up on the River Trent and float for 95secs, breaking the old record for raft formation of 30secs for 120 canoes.
Wednesday *May 28*	Kate Benjamin (24) leaves Land's End to ride 1400km on horseback to John O'Groats to raise money for African famine relief.
Thursday *May 29*	Oak Apple Day. The Queen is presented with an oak board-bound copy of the Domesday Book in a ceremony at the Royal Courts of Justice.
Friday *May 30*	From today, all new telephones will have push buttons instead of dials.
Saturday *May 31*	Football World Cup starts in Mexico. 1350 yachts race round the Isle of Wight. It's 96.54km and the winning boat *Paragon* finishes in 3hrs 55mins 30secs!

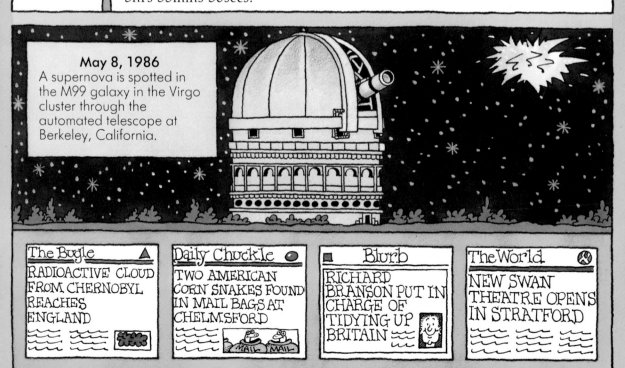

May 8, 1986
A supernova is spotted in the M99 galaxy in the Virgo cluster through the automated telescope at Berkeley, California.

The Bugle ▲
RADIOACTIVE CLOUD FROM CHERNOBYL REACHES ENGLAND

Daily Chuckle ●
TWO AMERICAN CORN SNAKES FOUND IN MAIL BAGS AT CHELMSFORD

■ Blurb
RICHARD BRANSON PUT IN CHARGE OF TIDYING UP BRITAIN

The World ✇
NEW SWAN THEATRE OPENS IN STRATFORD

June

Sunday June 1
Happy Birthday to Ripon in Yorkshire! It's 1100 years since King Alfred granted its first Royal Charter. Muscle Power World Championships are held at the Country Park, East Kilbride.

Monday June 2
Firemen in Nottingham can't practise in their training tower because of a pigeons' nest full of baby chicks.

Tuesday June 3
Mexico beat Belgium 2–1 in the first game of the World Cup. Delighted fans in the Aztec stadium in Mexico City give birth to the Mexican wave. A rare hen harrier's nest is found in the path of a new road being built at a Clyde submarine base. All work stops.

Wednesday June 4
An 82-year-old Teddy Bear is sold for £5,280 at Sotheby's in Chester. He is 76.2cm tall and originally cost 18s 9d (85p). The Derby is won by Shahrastani (11–2), owned by the Aga Khan.

Thursday June 5
The biggest ever cross-Channel car ferry, the 9517 tonne *Duc de Normandie*, makes her maiden trip from Portsmouth to Caen. She can carry 1500 passengers and 350 cars.

Friday June 6
Prince William joins the Automobile Association and becomes its 6,000,000th member!

Saturday June 7
The Milk Race ends, after 1770km and 13 days, on Waterloo Bridge in London. Joey McLoughlin and the ANC-Halford team win.

New Moon

Sunday June 8
A rare black-headed bunting from India is spotted at Clacton, Essex. Hundreds of twitchers flock to see it.

Monday June 9
A new wing is opened at the Royal Veterinary College near Potters Bar, Hertfordshire. It is named after Sefton, the cavalry horse who was badly injured in a bomb blast in 1982.

Tuesday June 10
Bob Geldof is made an honorary Knight of the British Empire. He can't call himself 'Sir Bob' because he is an Irish citizen, but can put KBE after his name instead.
Heavy snow in Cairngorms.

Wednesday June 11
The first official pollen count is issued today (very low—only 6). It's much later than usual because of the cold weather.

Thursday June 12
Two pandas called Ping Ping and Ming Ming land at Gatwick Airport from China, on their way to Dublin Zoo.

Friday June 13
A bad day for the poodle, Montravia Tommy-Gun, who won the Supreme Champion title at Cruft's in 1985: he has to give back one of his Kennel Club awards because his coat had been dyed!

June

Takes its name from Juno, the great Roman goddess of the Moon or from 'Juniores', the Latin word for young people, who were honoured this month. 'Zomer-maand' in Old Dutch (summer month) and 'Seremonath' in Old Saxon (dry month).

June 17: PO issues 4 new stamps to commemorate the 900th anniversary of the Domesday Book

The Hen Harrier's Tale

Once upon a time, at the beginning of June, 1986, a hen harrier built her nest and laid her eggs in the middle of a new road that was under construction at a submarine base on the Clyde. She was, of course, a protected species so the excavators and diggers screeched to a halt immediately. Experts were called in and a scheme was hatched which, it was hoped, would make everybody happy.

A copy of her nest was built on a wooden pallet (.42 sq m) and put on the original nesting site, carefully camouflaged with peat and heather. The real eggs were taken from the nest and moved to a safe place (at exactly the right temperature) while special chickens' eggs were arranged in the new nest. Then, VERY carefully, the new nest on the wooden pallet was moved 3.5m away from the road and up the hill. The hen harrier didn't seem to notice and came back to sit on the eggs quite happily after she'd had a quick stretch of her wings.

The same thing happened the next day and the next, as the nest, complete with Mum and her eggs, moved slowly up the hill at a rate of 3.5m each day. A few trees had to be chopped down, so that the hen harrier wouldn't notice the view changing too much, and an old stone wall had to come down too, but otherwise everything went smoothly and surely. At last, on June 15, the nest arrived at its final resting place 35m up the hill. The real eggs were then carefully replaced in the nest and the first chick hatched just after Midsummer's Day.

Saturday *June 14*	The rarest buttercup in Britain goes on show at a nature reserve at Badgeworth, Cheltenham. It's known as 'adder's tongue spearwort', but its proper name is Ranunculus Ophioglossifolius.
Sunday *June 15*	More than 20,000 cyclists pedal from London to Brighton in the annual Bike Race. Tanya Weston (10) is the 50,000th visitor to the Domesday Exhibition at the Public Records Office in Chancery Lane.
Monday *June 16*	Admiral Horatio Nelson gets ready to have his face cleaned, 51.82m above Trafalgar Square. It only happens once every 2yrs.
Tuesday *June 17*	A Penny Black stamp is sold for £3,200 at Christie's in London.
Wednesday *June 18*	Four sheep are put in the Lost Property Department at Cambridge railway station after they were found wandering on the tracks.
Thursday *June 19*	Fair Isle, between Orkney and Shetland, wins a Council of Europe award for its beauty and culture, as well as for being a Very Important Stopping-Off Point for migrating birds!
Friday *June 20*	Soviet cosmonauts Leonid Kizim and Vladimir Solovyov spend their 100th day in space on board the orbiting space station *Salyut-7*. Café Marron plants (see April 16) start growing roots at Kew.
Saturday *June 21*	Today's the longest day of the year: the Summer Solstice is at 4.30pm. Druids are banned from celebrating at Stonehenge. Happy birthday to Prince William! He's 4 today.
Sunday *June 22*	Viraf Mehta (27), wins the 19th National Scrabble Championship in London. Full Moon
Monday *June 23*	100th Wimbledon Lawn Tennis Championships opens. Yellow balls are used for the first time. Mrs Doris Eastwood, aged 52, from Weymouth, Dorset, becomes World Championship Town Crier at Wotton-under-Edge, Gloucs.
Tuesday *June 24*	Midsummer Day. It's too windy for *Virgin Atlantic Challenger II* to set off from the Ambrose Light, New York, in her attempt to break the Transatlantic speed record.
Wednesday *June 25*	Soviet cosmonauts Leonid Kizim and Vladimir Solovyov leave the space station *Salyut-7*, where they've lived since May, and travel back to the *Mir* space station on board their *Soyuz T15* spacecraft.

Thursday *June 26*	*Virgin Atlantic Challenger II* sets off from the Ambrose Light, New York, to cross the Atlantic: the record, set in 1952 by the liner *United States*, is 3days 10hrs 40mins. The Queen starts the Commonwealth Games relay run from Buckingham Palace.
Friday *June 27*	Hottest day of the year so far. It's 33°C on the Centre Court at Wimbledon. It's so hot that the judges at Portsmouth Crown Court take off their wigs.
Saturday *June 28*	The Fell and Rock Climbing Club of the English Lake District celebrates its 100th birthday on top of Napes Needle, Wastdale.
Sunday *June 29*	*Virgin Atlantic Challenger II* breaks the Transatlantic speed record by 2hrs 9mins. She completed the crossing in 3days 8hrs and 31mins. Argentina beats West Germany 3-2 and wins the World Cup in Mexico.

Hailstones 26mm in diameter fall on Jersey, CI
1.22m of flood water in Torquay

Monday *June 30*	The pier at Southend is sliced in two by a 655.32 tonne sludge ship. Seven people are stuck on the end and have to be rescued.

The Queen's Message, Carried in a Silver Baton from Buckingham Palace to Edinburgh, for the Opening of the XIII Commonwealth Games

This message of greetings has been brought to Edinburgh from Buckingham Palace by a relay of runners who have carried it 1750 miles through the Channel Islands, Wales, England and the Isle of Man, before crossing the Scottish border.

Although the organisation of the 3000 runners is quite a feat in itself, I would like to congratulate particularly the Organising Committee of the Games for their many years' work in making everything ready for this moment, the Official Opening of the XIII Commonwealth Games . . .

I am looking forward to joining you in a few days from now for what I know will be a great Festival of sport and fellowship.

Elizabeth

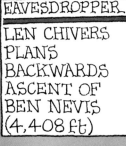

The Bugle ●
CHRISTMAS PUDDINGS LEAVE DERBYSHIRE FOR AUSTRALIA

Beaver ▲
FIRST FISH FINGER FACTORY CLOSES

EAVESDROPPER
LEN CHIVERS PLANS BACKWARDS ASCENT OF BEN NEVIS (4,408 ft)

Scribble ★
EUROPEAN PARLIAMENT VETOES FRENCH ATTEMPT TO CALL CHOCOLATE VEGOLATE

July

Tuesday July 1
Happy 25th birthday to the Princess of Wales! A Terek Sandpiper (rare wading bird that should be nesting in northern Russia) is spotted at Hauxley Nature Reserve, nr Amble, Northumberland.

Wednesday July 2
A survey carried out by Bristol University shows that there are 22 fox families living in Bath, 144 in Bournemouth and Poole and 683 in the West Midlands.

Thursday July 3
Prince Charles opens a new exhibition at the British Museum in London called 'Archaeology in Britain'. It stars Lindow Man, who was found in a peat bog near Wilmslow, Cheshire. He is more than 2000 years old and has been specially freeze-dried.

Friday July 4
American Independence Day. The Statue of Liberty celebrates her 100th birthday today. The Tour de France cycle race starts in Paris.

Saturday July 5
A 20.73m corn circle appears in a field in the Devil's Punchbowl, nr Alresford, Hampshire. Navratilova beats Mandlikova 7–6, 6–3, to win the ladies' final at Wimbledon for the 5th year running.

Sunday July 6
Boris Becker, only 17, beats Ivan Lendl 6–4, 6–3, 7–5, and becomes the youngest-ever Men's Wimbledon Champion.
New Moon

Monday July 7
According to the World Population Institute, there are 5,000,000,000 people in the world today. There have never been so many people on Earth before!

Tuesday July 8
A white-throated Capuchin monkey called Cleopatra is born at Kilverstone Wildlife Park, nr Thetford, Norfolk. Her Mum is called Shy-Anne and her Dad is called Frank.

Wednesday July 9
Deep-sea divers set off from Wood's Hole, Massachusetts, to inspect the wreck of the *Titanic*, which sank in 1912. It's lying at the bottom of the sea about 644km south of Newfoundland.

Thursday July 10
Fish are dying in the River Thames between Battersea and Putney in London—especially eels, flounder and dace—because there's not enough oxygen in the water. Fresh water has to be pumped over Teddington weir at three times its normal rate!

Friday July 11
24 hot-air balloons take off from Southampton Common at the start of the International Great Southern Balloon Race.

Saturday July 12
An English springer spaniel called Ziggy patrols Westminster Abbey: he'll be on sniffer dog duty until July 23, when Prince Andrew marries Sarah Ferguson.

July

Happy 100th Birthday to the Statue of Liberty!

The Statue of Liberty's 100th birthday party lasts for four days in New York Harbour. In preparation for such a great event, she has had her nose rebuilt and a spot on her eye removed. The spikes on her crown have been repaired and her torch has a nice new goldleaf flame. She's been strengthened, inside and out, with the help of 12,000 rivets and 1825 steel bars. The arm that holds the torch and one shoulder have been reinforced and there's a new viewing platform with bigger windows inside her crown. Her insides have been thoroughly cleaned with sodium bicarbonate and her outside with a special water bath.

President Reagan starts the festivities by unveiling the Statue electronically. A laser beam is sent half a mile across the harbour to switch on the coloured lights. Taking part in the celebrations are a 500-strong marching band, 1000 tap dancers, an 800-voice choir and 5000 birds of peace!

Some Vital Statistics
Together with her pedestal, Liberty is almost as tall as a football field is long (92.694m).
She weighs 225 tonnes—about the same as 45 large elephants.
Her mouth is a metre wide
Her fingernail is bigger than this book (250 × 190mm).
Her hand is as long as three people laid end to end (5m).

P.S. Anybody who's anybody in New York this weekend wears a bright green crown with seven spikes. They're made of foam, cost $3 (about £2) each, and are just like Liberty's headdress—except a bit smaller and without the viewing platform!

Sunday *July 13*	Nigel Mansell wins the British Grand Prix at Brands Hatch. Jake wins the Supreme Champion title at Scruffts Show for mongrels at Orpington, Kent.
Monday *July 14*	The Royal Geographic Society launches an expedition called '90° South', retracing Amundsen's journey to the South Pole in 1911. A team of 4 will travel 2,896km on skis from the Bay of Whales to the South Pole.
Tuesday *July 15*	St Swithin's Day: if it rains today, it will rain for 40 days! Hottest day of the year so far in Central London—it's at least 29.5°C.
Wednesday *July 16*	2000 lobsters escape when a lorry turns over at Bere Regis, Dorset. Soviet cosmonauts Leonid Kizim and Vladimir Solovyov return to Earth after 4 months in space.
Thursday *July 17*	Charlie Chaplin's hat and cane are sold for £15,000 at Christie's in London.
Friday *July 18*	Three South American rhea ostrich chicks, hatched at the Springhill Wildfowl Park at Forest Row, Sussex, have to be fed with meal worms every two hours.
Saturday *July 19*	100 snails compete in the World Snail Racing Championships at Congham, Norfolk. *Solarium Sal*, owned by Amy Gooding (5), streaks over the 33.02cm course in 2mins 51secs and wins the silver tankard.
Sunday *July 20*	Lenny Denton (47) sets a new World Record for pushing a 101.6kg wheelbarrow from London to John O'Groats, then to Land's End and back to London in 50 days.
Monday *July 21*	Prince Andrew and Sarah Ferguson's wedding cake arrives safely at Buckingham Palace from Torpoint, Cornwall, where it was made by the Royal Navy's Supply School at *HMS Raleigh*. An identical cake travels in convoy in case there's an accident. Full Moon
Tuesday *July 22*	A portrait of the largest pig ever bred in Britain is sold for £15,400 at Sotheby's. It is a Gloucester Old Spot, which weighed 639.564kg.
Wednesday *July 23*	Prince Andrew marries Sarah Ferguson in Westminster Abbey: the ceremony starts at 11.30am and the worldwide TV audience is 5,000,000.
Thursday *July 24*	The Duke of Edinburgh opens the XIII Commonwealth Games at Meadowbank Stadium, Edinburgh.

Friday *July 25*	Scientists who re-measured Mont Blanc this month say that it is 4,808.52m high. That's 1.22m higher than when it was first calculated at the end of the last century!
Saturday *July 26*	Members of the Sealed Knot re-enact the Civil War Battle of Radcot near Faringdon, Oxfordshire. It was originally fought in 1645.
Sunday *July 27*	The Tour de France ends in Paris. It is won for the first time by an American, Greg Lemond. World Wheelchair Games open at Stoke Mandeville, Bucks.
Monday *July 28*	Joanna, a red-kneed bird-eating tarantula helps to launch Creepy Crawly Week at London Zoo. The first potatoes arrived in Britain 400 years ago today. 4.47mm of rain at Nantmor, N. Wales
Tuesday *July 29*	John Swain (62) from Brookham's Park, Hertfordshire, becomes Express Dairy Milkman of the Year.
Wednesday *July 30*	A British expedition leaves England for Tibet: it's heading for the North East ridge of Everest which has never been climbed!
Thursday *July 31*	The last Royal Navy sailmaker at Portsmouth, CPO Jack Corser, retires. It's the end of a 400 year-old tradition, dating back to Henry VIII.

July 15: PO issues 5 stamps to celebrate the Commonwealth Games in Edinburgh

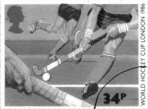

July 23: The wedding of Prince Andrew and Sarah Ferguson. The royal wedding dress has a train 5.33m long, there are more than 24,000 rose petals in the confetti, and the cake weighs 109kg. The happy couple will be known as the Duke and Duchess of York. The PO issues two stamps on July 22 to mark the occasion.

August

Friday *August 1*	D is the new letter at the beginning of car number plates. Yorkshire Day is celebrated in Barnsley with a 13.3sq m Yorkshire pudding: it contains 600 eggs and 120kg of flour.
Saturday *August 2*	Closing ceremony of the Commonwealth Games in Edinburgh: A Scouts' Jamboree at Plymouth is cancelled after tents are torn down by gale-force winds and driving rain.
Sunday *August 3*	Torrential rain in SE England and Wales. It's so wet at the 107th National Eisteddfod of Wales in Fishguard that some ceremonies have to be postponed.
Monday *August 4*	Happy 86th birthday to HRH Queen Elizabeth the Queen Mother! Mrs Julie Tullis (47) reaches the top of K2. It's the second highest peak in the Himalayas at 8610.6m.
Tuesday *August 5*	Princess Anne rides her first winner, Gulfland, as an amateur jockey in the 3.45 at Redcar. New Moon
Wednesday *August 6*	The Advanced Turbo-prop (ATP) airliner makes its maiden 2½hr flight from Woodford Aerodrome, Manchester.
Thursday *August 7*	A 1566.3kg Great White Shark is caught off Montauk, Long Island, USA. It's 508cm long and is the largest shark ever caught by line!
Friday *August 8*	Southend Pier, which was sliced in two at the end of June, is mended. A 7.62m inflatable kangaroo floats across the English Channel at 3,048m, attached to six helium balloons.
Saturday *August 9*	A giant oil rig that cost £50,000,000 to build is named 'Mr Mac' by the Queen at Greenock on the Clyde. She wets its 17,780 tonne platform with a litre of whisky instead of champagne.
Sunday *August 10*	40th Edinburgh Festival opens. Jim Cropper from Rossendale, Lancs, and his dog, Cap, win the English National Sheepdog trials at Beadnell, near Berwick-upon-Tweed.
Monday *August 11*	The Queen climbs 34.75m up 152 steps to the top of the lighthouse at Ardnamurchan in Argyll. Afterwards, she has a cup of tea with the lighthouse keeper's wife, Mrs Nan Hardie.
Tuesday *August 12*	'Sunrider', a solar-powered car built at Cardiff University, arrives in Madrid after travelling 2252.6km from Athens at an average speed of 32.18km/h.

Wednesday *August 13*	Simon Bornhoft (21) sets out from Weymouth to windsurf to Brighton: he's trying to beat the endurance record of 87hrs 33mins!
Thursday *August 14*	Crayfish Day in Sweden. HRH Queen Elizabeth the Queen Mother swallows a fishbone and is rushed to Aberdeen Royal Infirmary in Scotland.
Friday *August 15*	120 competitors take off in hot air balloon race to mark the start of the 2nd Bristol International Fiesta from Ashton Court at 6.30am.
Saturday *August 16*	A 20th century Viking longship invades Lundy Island in the Bristol Channel to raise money for the lifeboat at Clovelly, North Devon.
Sunday *August 17*	Simon Bornhoft arrives in Brighton: he beats the world windsurfing endurance record by 3hrs. He spent 90hrs 45mins and 55secs on his board between Weymouth and Brighton.
Monday *August 18*	Reykjavik, the capital of Iceland, holds its 200th birthday party: there are fireworks, a fun run and a cake 182.8m long!

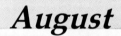

August

Named in honour of the Roman Emperor Augustus, whose lucky month it was. Also known as 'harvest month' and 'weed month'.

'Sunrider'

The 'Sunrider' solar-powered car weighs 90.8kg and has 300 solar cells glued to its body. During its journey across Europe this summer it went more slowly than expected because the temperature was too high!

August 19: PO issues a new stamp to mark the 32nd Commonwealth Parliamentary Conference

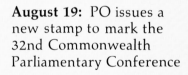

How Everest Got Its Name

Mount Everest, the highest peak in the world, used to be known as Peak XV. Then, in 1865, it was named after the Surveyor General for India, who happened to be called Sir George Everest. He also carried out something called the Great Trigonometrical Survey of India.

Tuesday *August 19*	Two members of the Dangerous Sports Club try to roll down the river Thames inside a gigantic plastic bubble as high as five double decker buses: they sink within a few seconds. Full Moon
Wednesday *August 20*	Royal Marines set a new World Record for parachute stacking over Dunkeswell Airfield in Devon. 24 parachutists stand on each other's shoulders.
Thursday *August 21*	Hamley's of Regent Street, the most famous toy shop in the world, is sold for £30,000,000. John Adams (8) from Ashfordby, Leics, gets a Grade B pass in 'O' Level Maths.
Friday *August 22*	Five large teddy bears fall off a lorry on the M3 at Fleet, Hants, and are taken into custody at Basingstoke police station.
Saturday *August 23*	Firefighting planes drop water bombs on the worst forest fire of the year on the Cote d'Azur, France. 5000 hectares destroyed.
Sunday *August 24*	The first Super Prix motor race through the streets of Birmingham has to be stopped at the half-way point because of torrential rain. Typhoon Wayne hits Taiwan
Monday *August 25*	Bank Holiday. Geoff Cooper, from Mere, Wilts, sets off to row round the world from Coverack, Cornwall, in a 4.88m boat called the *Water Rat*.
Tuesday *August 26*	Hurricane Charley brings storms that kill 5 people in Britain and 6 in Ireland. It's the busiest day ever for the AA—there are nearly 13,500 breakdown calls!
Wednesday *August 27*	A UN survey shows that jellyfish have almost disappeared from the western and central Mediterranean.
Thursday *August 28*	Fatima Whitbread throws a javelin 77.45m at the European Athletics Championships, Stuttgart. She's the first woman ever to throw a javelin more than 76.2m.
Friday *August 29*	Geoff Cooper, who set out to row round the world at the beginning of the week, is rescued after breaking his wrist. The first World Games for Disabled Youth start in Nottingham.
Saturday *August 30*	The British expedition to the North East ridge of Everest establishes its base camp at 5029.2m on the Rongbuk glacier.
Sunday *August 31*	Chris Bromham breaks his own World Record for motorcycle jumping at the Royal Victoria Dock, London: he leaps 73.6m over 20 trucks.

September

Monday *September 1*	Arnold Fewell, who weighs 141kg and is Head of School Dinners for North Yorkshire, starts a sponsored slim.
Tuesday *September 2*	The 15-storey high Dutch Viking hot-air balloon lands in a cornfield in Holland and sets a new World Record for crossing the Atlantic in 51hrs 14mins.
Wednesday *September 3*	A new drill is tried out on the Great Pyramid of Giza, Egypt, in a search for secret chambers and the missing mummy of King Cheops.
Thursday *September 4*	European Grass Ski Championships at Butser Hill, nr Petersfield, Hampshire. New Moon
Friday *September 5*	Les Dawson switches on the Blackpool Illuminations at 9pm. They cost £1,250,000 and weigh nearly 712 tonnes. Altogether there are 375,000 light bulbs and 120.675km of wire and cable.
Saturday *September 6*	The 14.02m *Kyrenia II* sets sail from Piraeus, nr Athens: she's a full-size copy of a Greek merchant ship which was sunk by pirates off Cyprus 2200 years ago.
Sunday *September 7*	Mrs Susan Knowles (23) blows up a 21-storey tower block called Highworth Point in Hackney Wick with 181.6kg of explosives. She won it as a prize in a raffle!
Monday *September 8*	The National Dairy Council says that 284,480 tonnes of cheese were eaten in Britain in the last year. We each eat 3.59kg a year!
Tuesday *September 9*	RSPB says that it's been a terrible year for Arctic terns in Orkney and Shetland: hardly any eggs have hatched. Most of the terns are flying off to their winter grounds in the Antarctic now.
Wednesday *September 10*	A pet shop in Leamington Spa is fined £200 for selling Great Crested or Warty Newts at 85p each. They are a protected species.
Thursday *September 11*	Barry Kirk from Port Talbot, West Glam, starts a Beanathon at the Aberfan Hotel. He's trying to break the World Record for sitting in a bath of cold baked beans!
Friday *September 12*	A dolphin which was trapped in the River Severn at Longney, Gloucs., for nearly a week is caught and driven in a van to the Bristol Channel. It is set free and swims off.
Saturday *September 13*	Hundreds of people in Paris demonstrate outside the pets' cemetery at Asnières, which is threatened with closure. There are 2700 graves there, including Rin Tin Tin's.

Sunday *September 14*	The Duke of York is voted one of the Ten Best Dressed Men by the Menswear Association. So are Richard Branson and Cliff Richard.
Monday *September 15*	Happy 2nd birthday, Prince Harry! Barry Kirk finishes his Beanathon. He sat in a bath of cold baked beans for 100 hours!
Tuesday *September 16*	Terry Waite launches an appeal for peace by going up in a hot-air balloon from Trafalgar Square. People all over the world stand in silence for a minute and think about PEACE.
Wednesday *September 17*	Matthew Parker (16) from Tickshill, nr Doncaster, becomes Young Engineer of the Year with a new muscle-stretching machine.
Thursday *September 18*	The Ministry of Agriculture declares West Dorset and parts of Somerset and Devon warble-fly-infected areas. Full Moon
Friday *September 19*	A new puzzle called Rubik's Magic is launched at the Budapest Trade Fair by the Hungarian inventor Erno Rubik. It's made up of 8 flat sections joined by movable hinges that have 45 angles.
Saturday *September 20*	World Gurning Championships are held at the Egremont Crab Fair in Cumbria: the person who can pull the most horrible face wins!
Sunday *September 21*	Great Billingsgate Fish Fair. Horseman's Sunday in Hyde Park, London: the vicar holds a service on horseback in the forecourt of St John's Church with about 100 horses in the congregation.
Monday *September 22*	The Prime Minister, Mrs Thatcher, is presented with a scroll at 10 Downing Street by Zhiang Aiping, the Chinese Defence Minister. The verse says (in Chinese): 'It's easy to be a starter but are you a sticker too, It's easy enough to begin a job, it's harder to see it through.'
Tuesday *September 23*	The new Dundonald International Ice Bowl in Belfast is opened today: it cost £4,500,000 and is the largest ice rink in the UK!
Wednesday *September 24*	Mount Etna erupts in Sicily: a new crack opens on the North East summit and a black cloud of volcanic ash floats into the sky.
Thursday *September 25*	Official opening of the 32nd Commonwealth Parliamentary Conference in Westminster Hall, London. More than 60 firemen are called to put out a blaze at the Bank of England at 3am.
Friday *September 26*	Frank Butter becomes British Champion Lock Keeper: he looks after 5 locks and a bridge on the Shropshire Union Canal near Market Drayton.

September

This was the seventh month when the year used to start in March. Also known as the month of reaping, 'barley month' and the 'holy month'.

1986: Year of the Bat

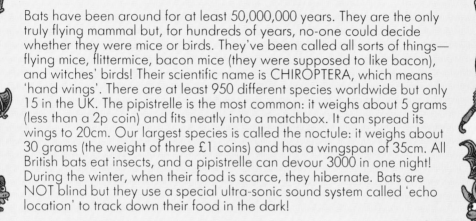

Bats have been around for at least 50,000,000 years. They are the only truly flying mammal but, for hundreds of years, no-one could decide whether they were mice or birds. They've been called all sorts of things—flying mice, flittermice, bacon mice (they were supposed to like bacon), and witches' birds! Their scientific name is CHIROPTERA, which means 'hand wings'. There are at least 950 different species worldwide but only 15 in the UK. The pipistrelle is the most common: it weighs about 5 grams (less than a 2p coin) and fits neatly into a matchbox. It can spread its wings to 20cm. Our largest species is called the noctule: it weighs about 30 grams (the weight of three £1 coins) and has a wingspan of 35cm. All British bats eat insects, and a pipistrelle can devour 3000 in one night! During the winter, when their food is scarce, they hibernate. Bats are NOT blind but they use a special ultra-sonic sound system called 'echo location' to track down their food in the dark!

British Bats

Greater Horseshoe bat	Serotine bat
Lesser Horseshoe bat	Daubenton's bat
Noctule bat	Whiskered bat
Leisler's bat	Brandt's bat
Pipistrelle bat	Natterer's bat
Brown Long-Eared bat	Barbastelle bat
Grey Long-Eared bat	Bechstein's bat
Mouse-Eared bat	

Artificial Bat Caves

The artificial bat cave at Brent is 10m long and is dug into a 2m high clay bank. It's made up of three main sections: an entrance tunnel, a main chamber and a smaller rear chamber. There's plenty of room for hundreds of bats to hibernate at the same time. Another purpose-built bat cave is also under way at Monkton Chalk Pit, Kent. (By the time it's opened on Oct 18, mosquitoes, fungus gnats and hoverflies have already moved in to hibernate!)

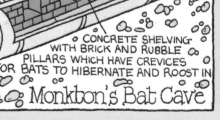

VENTILATION PIPE FROM THE CAVE

CONCRETE FILLED SANDBAGS

CHALK SOIL

CONCRETE SHELVING WITH BRICK AND RUBBLE PILLARS WHICH HAVE CREVICES FOR BATS TO HIBERNATE AND ROOST IN

1·5m DIAMETER CONCRETE PIPES FORMING MAIN CAVE STRUCTURE

Monkton's Bat Cave

Saturday *September 27*	Britain's first artificial bat cave is opened in Brent. It's called a hibernaculum and can house hundreds of bats at a time!
Sunday *September 28*	*Sunday Times* Fun Run in Hyde Park, London. An African Green Monkey called Zacherie, who escaped from his home near Chippenham, Wilts, eleven weeks ago, is spotted on the M4.
Monday *September 29*	Guide Dog Week begins today. An earthquake on the west coast of Scotland at 2.33am lasts 20secs and measures 3.5 on the Richter Scale. The epicentre is at Loch Linnhe, near Oban.
Tuesday *September 30*	Today is the last day for entries to next year's London Marathon, which will be held on May 10. 

September 16: PO issues 5 new stamps on the history of the RAF

LORD DOWDING / HURRICANE

LORD TEDDER / TYPHOON

LORD TRENCHARD / DH 9A

LORD PORTAL / MOSQUITO

SIR ARTHUR HARRIS / LANCASTER

Wacky September Weather

Earthquake in N. Cornwall measures 3 on the Richter Scale

Snow showers in N. Scotland

Earthquake in Greece measures 6.2 on the Richter Scale

25°C at Newcastle-upon-Tyne

RICHTER SCALE

Daily Trumpet
LOCUST SWARMS THREATEN FOOD CROPS IN AFRICA

The Herald
NEW JAPANESE CAR FACTORY OPENS IN WASHINGTON, CO DURHAM

Daily Gossip
SNAKES AND LIZARDS GET 10 NEW SPECIAL SITES IN WAREHAM, DORSET

Bleet
STEVE CRAM BREAKS UK MILE RECORD IN 3 MINS 49.49 SECS

October

Wednesday *October 1*	A Scottish yachtswoman called Anne Miller sails into Campbeltown two years after leaving Bermuda to cross the Atlantic.
Thursday *October 2*	You can tell the time by the four-faced clock on Brighton station for the first time in more than a year: it's been cleaned and more than 101.6kg of dirt was removed! New Moon
Friday *October 3*	Start of the Jewish New Year. Over 3 tonnes of mixed biscuits block the road for 7hrs at Markeaton, Derbyshire, after a lorry turns over.
Saturday *October 4*	The torch, which left New York on September 16 on the First Earth Run, to celebrate the UN's Year of Peace and the 40th anniversary of UNICEF, arrives in London.
Sunday *October 5*	30 people who don't have jobs leave Jarrow on Tyneside to walk to London: it's the 50th anniversary of the original 1936 Jarrow Crusade when 200 jobless men marched to London.
Monday *October 6*	A 3.86kg salmon is caught in the Thames at Boulters Lock nr Reading by Nigel Leck from Maidenhead. It's the first salmon to be caught in the middle bit of the river for more than a century.
Tuesday *October 7*	A new national daily newspaper is born today: it's called *The Independent* and it costs 25p. 22.6°C at Hoddesdon, Herts
Wednesday *October 8*	A famous painting by Rembrandt, which was stolen from the Dulwich Picture Gallery, is found in the left luggage department at Munich railway station in West Germany. The portrait has been stolen 4 times in 16 yrs!
Thursday *October 9*	Traffic is held up for 30 minutes at Odcombe, nr Yeovil, Somerset, while a cow gives birth to a calf in the middle of the road.
Friday *October 10*	There are celebrations in London tonight to mark the 100th birthday of the Dinner Jacket.
Saturday *October 11*	Mother Teresa (76) escapes unhurt when a 'plane in which she is flying crashes in central Tanzania. Special 'Bats Afternoon' at the Queen Elizabeth Hall, London.
Sunday *October 12*	The Queen starts a six-day State Visit to China: it's the first time a British monarch has ever been there.
Monday *October 13*	The Queen is entertained at a banquet in Peking's Great Hall of the People. On the menu are sea slugs, chicken soup with jasmine blossoms and succulent shark's fin.

Tuesday *October 14*	Two peregrine falcons are employed at Dublin Airport to keep seagulls away from aircraft—they're a safety hazard.
Wednesday *October 15*	All official engagements are cancelled in Ramsbury, Wilts, today as a mark of respect for the 17th century elm tree which is cut down in the village square. It died from Dutch Elm Disease.
Thursday *October 16*	British Coal officially opens the first new pit in Scotland for 20 years. It's the Castlehill Colliery, 4.8km east of Alloa.
Friday *October 17*	You can see a total eclipse of the Moon from all over the country between 7.41pm and 8.55pm this evening. Barcelona, Spain, wins the bid to host the 1992 Olympic Games. Full Moon
Saturday *October 18*	The Taunton Annual Illuminated Carnival and Cider Barrel Race.
Sunday *October 19*	The first snow of winter in England falls on Holme Moss Moor in the Peak District.
Monday *October 20*	The last steamship crossing of the Atlantic starts today: the *QE2* leaves New York for Southampton. She will be refitted with a new diesel electric system.
Tuesday *October 21*	An Australian, Nicholas Feteris (25), is fined $100 (£70) for parachuting 91.44m from the Statue of Liberty in New York without a permit.
Wednesday *October 22*	The Queen gives her autograph to Raymond Tung (8), in Hong Kong—'Elizabeth R 1986'.
Thursday *October 23*	A pair of crowned eagles fly back to Zimbabwe by jet: they were originally smuggled into Britain as eggs. 3000 bee keepers buzz round the Honey Show at Porchester Hall, London.
Friday *October 24*	The racehorse Dancing Brave, who won the Prix de l'Arc de Triomphe earlier this month, flies from Gatwick to Los Angeles (11hrs). He will spend 28hrs in quarantine once he gets there, before he races in the Breeders' Cup at Santa Anita.
Saturday *October 25*	World Bagpipes Championships are held at Blair Castle in Scotland: Iain MacFadyen, from the Kyle of Lochalsh, wins for the fourth time.
Sunday *October 26*	Clocks go back by 1hr tonight when Summer Time ends. An artificial bat cave opens at Monkton, Kent.

Monday *October 27*	World Day of Prayer for Peace. Religious leaders from all over the world join Pope John Paul II for prayers at Assisi, Italy.
Tuesday *October 28*	Sir Allan Davis, Lord Mayor of London, launches the annual Poppy Appeal.
Wednesday *October 29*	Mrs Thatcher, the Prime Minister, opens the last stretch of the M25 motorway round London at 11.15 this morning.
Thursday *October 30*	Father Christmas arrives at Hamley's, Regent Street. The Jonagold apple, a cross between a Jonathan and a Golden Delicious, is voted most eatable apple of the year by the judges at Marden Fruit Fair.
Friday *October 31*	Hallowe'en. Colchester Oyster Feast at the Town Hall, Colchester. A glue tanker turns over on the A355 at Slough, Berkshire and causes an 8km jam.

October

 This was the eighth month in the old Roman calendar when the year started in March. It's also been known as 'wine month' and 'month of the winter moon'.

XXII World Conker Championship

On October 12, 1986, 64 people take part in the 22nd World Conker Championship. They play on the village green at Ashton, nr Oundle, Northants. About 600 conkers are used this year—all carefully collected by the Conker Committee and graded according to shape and size. Holes are made in them with an electric drill and leather bootlaces threaded through. Contestants are divided into four sections and then each pair in each section tosses a coin to see who takes first strike. The game is played with each player having three strikes at his opponent's conker in turn until one conker is broken. Gradually, the players are knocked out until there are four left in the semi-finals and then two in the finals. Charlie Bray (68) of Whitchurch, Hants, wins this year's title.

The Independent
'It is, are you?'

The Independent is the first completely new national broadsheet to be born for 40 years. It's got 32 pages which are printed at plants around the country using the computer-based new technology. On the first day, Oct. 7, 650,080 copies are printed.

November

Saturday *November 1*	Diwali, the festival of light, in India: £4,000,000 of fireworks are set off in Delhi this weekend! New Moon
Sunday *November 2*	367 veteran cars take part in the annual London to Brighton run—including the oldest car in the world, an 1886 Daimler.
Monday *November 3*	The first complete Chinese library service in Britain opens in Manchester.
Tuesday *November 4*	The inner circle of stones at Stonehenge is re-opened: visitors will be allowed in on Tuesdays and Fridays until the end of February.
Wednesday *November 5*	Bonfire Night. Site of Special Scientific Interest is declared near Salisbury, Wilts. It is the home of the rare Sehirus Dubius Bug.
Thursday *November 6*	Tracy Nelson, born at the beginning of the year in Chesterfield, finally gets her birth certificate. It's taken a long time because she's got 140 Christian names which had to go on an extra page.
Friday *November 7*	The annual parade in Red Square, Moscow celebrates the 69th anniversary of the Revolution in 1917. A model fun fair, made of 20,000 pieces of Meccano with 1000 light bulbs, goes on show at the Model, Hobby and Games World Exhibition in London.
Saturday *November 8*	Lord Mayor's Show in London. Father Christmas arrives at Browns department store, Chester, in a vintage Rolls Royce.
Sunday *November 9*	Remembrance Sunday: two minutes silence at 11am to remember those that died in two World Wars.
Monday *November 10*	Chemicals which were spilled into the River Rhine in Germany on Nov 3 reach Amsterdam. Eels, pike, perch, trout—even river fleas—have been wiped out. 16.7°C at Hoddesdon, Herts
Tuesday *November 11*	Martinmas—traditionally the festival of the beginning of winter. Scientists say that a HUGE raindrop, 8mm in diameter, has been found in a cloud just east of Hawaii!
Wednesday *November 12*	Dr Richard Crane (32) is named Outstanding Young Person of the World in a ceremony in Japan. He ran through the Himalayas to raise money for charity.
Thursday *November 13*	A memorial to Edmund Halley is unveiled in the South Cloister at Westminster Abbey at 5.30pm. It's made out of Welsh slate and is in the shape of a comet.

Friday *November 14*	Glasgow is named as European City of Culture 1990. *Torrential rain in west Wales. Hailstones 20–22mm in diameter fall at Lerwick, Shetlands*
Saturday *November 15*	World Budgerigar Championships are held at Doncaster Race Course and Exhibition Centre.
Sunday *November 16*	The prophet Muhamad's birthday. The four-day 2413.5km Lombard RAC rally starts at Bath. Full Moon 
Monday *November 17*	A priceless bronze Celtic shield goes on show at the British Museum. It dates from about 400BC and was found in a gravel pit at Chertsey, Surrey. *Best night of the year for the Leonid meteor showers!*
Tuesday *November 18*	The Flora and Fauna Preservation Society launches a SAVE OUR SNAKES campaign. 

November

This was the ninth month in the old Roman calendar when the year started in March. It's also been known as 'wind month', 'slaughter month' and 'the month of blood'.

November 18:   PO issues the Christmas stamps

The Glastonbury Thorn — 12ᴾ
The Glastonbury Thorn — 13ᴾ

The Tanad Valley Plygain — 18ᴾ

The Hebrides Tribute — 22ᴾ

The Dewsbury Church Knell — 31ᴾ

The Hereford Boy Bishop — 34ᴾ

Crescendo ▲
BAKED BEAN HARVEST IN US AND CANADA RUINED BY RAIN

Blabber Mouth
KANGAROO PLAGUE IN QUEENS-LAND

Whoop ●
ROYAL GREENWICH OBSERVATORY TO MOVE FROM SUSSEX TO CAMBRIDGE

Hedgehog ▲
HIGH WINDS AND HEAVY RAINS FORCE BRITISH EXPEDITION TO ABANDON ATTEMPT ON GANKAR PUNSUM

Wednesday *November 19*	An earth tremor shakes North Wales between 1 and 1.15am this morning. It measures 2.7 on the Richter Scale. Gale-force winds and torrential rain in the south.
Thursday *November 20*	A new 10.67m oak tree is planted in the square at Ramsbury, Wiltshire, to replace the famous 300 year-old elm that was cut down earlier this year.
Friday *November 21*	Lundy Island in the Bristol Channel becomes the first marine nature reserve in Britain. Tornado at Selsey, W. Sussex.
Saturday *November 22*	Alan Dean wins the national singles Tiddlywinks championship at Southampton. Wheelclamping in central London is stopped for a fortnight—until December 1, when the service will be privatised.
Sunday *November 23*	The annual meeting of the Channel Swimming Association is held in Folkestone. It's been the busiest year ever for cross-Channel swimming: more than 70 attempts were made. 21 solo swimmers and 19 relay teams got across!
Monday *November 24*	1200 pupils at Garth Hill Comprehensive, Bracknell, Berks, are offered breakfast before starting lessons today.
Tuesday *November 25*	The Pope visits the Lone Pine Koala Sanctuary during his visit to Brisbane, Australia.
Wednesday *November 26*	A 124,000,000 year-old dinosaur, found in a Surrey claypit, is given its official name today. It's called *Baryonyx Walkeri*, which means 'a heavy clawed creature found by Mr Walker'. It weighed 2.032 tonnes and had 128 teeth (instead of the usual 64) and was found at Smokejack Pit, Dorking.
Thursday *November 27*	Three North Sea oilfields (Piper, Claymore and Tartan) are shut down after an oilslick 8.045km long and 3.218km wide is spotted in the North Sea.
Friday *November 28*	Topping-out ceremony of the new South Transept roof at York Minster. Dumfries railway station, in the Scottish Borders, wins the Best Station 1986 Award.
Saturday *November 29*	You can hear the bells of Peterborough Cathedral ringing for the first time in 60 years! A new peal of 14 bells is dedicated today.
Sunday *November 30*	A racing pigeon called Peter Pan is sold for £41,000 in Belgium—a World Record price! An 89kg St Bernard called Schnorbitz wins the Pro Dogs Pet of the Year gold medal.

December

Monday *December 1*	St Andrew's Day. Sir John Harvey-Jones, Chairman of ICI, is named Businessman of the Year in London. New Moon
Tuesday *December 2*	A 15 month-old steer, called Bruno, wins the Supreme Championship at the Royal Smithfield Show, Earl's Court. He weighs 563kg.
Wednesday *December 3*	Addingham School, near Bradford, is awarded a rare gold star by Her Majesty's Inspectors of Schools. Nine sketches from Lewis Carroll's *Alice's Adventures in Wonderland* are sold for £187,000 at Christie's in London.
Thursday *December 4*	Ceremony of the Christmas Cheeses at the Royal Hospital, Chelsea. The National Dairy Council gives 136.2kg of cheese each year to the pensioners. 15°C at Mansfield, Notts
Friday *December 5*	The only known copy of a miniature book printed in 1775 is sold at Sotheby's in London for £8,800. It's called *Tom Thumb's Play Book.* TOM THUMBS PLAY BOOK
Saturday *December 6*	The Royal Mail hires an extra 3500 vans and lorries to cope with Christmas rush. Also 30,000 extra post people!
Sunday *December 7*	Thousands of tonnes of mud block the road from Ballycastle to Belmullet in Co Mayo: a peat bog has shifted after a week of heavy rain!
Monday *December 8*	Royal Christmas trees from the Queen's estate at Sandringham go on sale for the first time. They cost 80p a foot (£2.62 a metre) if the bottom is sawn off, or £1 a foot (£3.28 a metre) with roots.
Tuesday *December 9*	A new museum of 19th century art opens in Paris. Created out of an old railway station on the Left Bank, it's called the Musée d'Orsay.
Wednesday *December 10*	The longest motorway tunnel in Britain is opened today. It runs for 1.207km underneath Hatfield, and is part of a new section of the A1 between Roestock and Stanborough.
Thursday *December 11*	The Christmas Tree lights are switched on in Trafalgar Square, London, by the Norwegian Ambassador. The Middleham Jewel, a gold locket that was found in North Yorkshire, is sold for £1.3m at Sotheby's, London. It dates from the reign of Richard III.
Friday *December 12*	The Queen's adopted Bewick's Swan, 'Coronation', settles down at the Wildfowl Trust, Slimbridge, Gloucs. She's just arrived back for her ninth winter after flying 3701km from the Arctic.

Saturday *December 13*	The Royal Navy's new 8636-tonne landing vessel *Sir Galahad* is launched on the River Tyne, replacing the ship lost in the Falklands conflict.
Sunday *December 14*	Twin-engine aircraft *Voyager 4* takes off from the Mojave Desert, California, in an attempt to fly round the world without stopping to refuel.
Monday *December 15*	Nearly 120,000,000 cards, letters and parcels are posted today—an all-time record!
Tuesday *December 16*	Beginning of the Mince Pie season. Typhoon Marge, blowing at 137km/h, helps *Voyager 4* (see 14 December) on her way. She's ahead of schedule, 112.63km north of the island of Saipan in the Pacific Ocean, at 6.00pm. Full Moon
Wednesday *December 17*	Mrs Thatcher, the Prime Minister, sends 'Don't Drink and Drive' messages on special gold scrolls from London to the other 11 EC capitals.
Thursday *December 18*	The House of Lords breaks up for Christmas. Term doesn't start again until January 12! Children of Courage Awards at Westminster Abbey, London.
Friday *December 19*	The House of Commons breaks up for Christmas. They won't be back until January 12 either! Absolutely the last day for posting first class Christmas cards and letters.
Saturday *December 20*	Fourteen pilot whales, some weighing more than a tonne, beach themselves on the Isle of Sanday in the Orkneys.
Sunday *December 21*	The shortest day of the year. A Christmas hamper is helicoptered in for the last time to the Skerries lighthouse, 14.48km north of Holyhead. It's being automated next February.
Monday *December 22*	The Santa Steam Special takes children on the Watercress Line from Alresford, Hampshire, to see Father Christmas in Alton. The locomotive was built in 1889!
Tuesday *December 23*	*Voyager 4* lands at Edwards Air Force Base, California, after flying non-stop round the world without refuelling in 9days 3mins and 44secs.
Wednesday *December 24*	Special cheap Christmas 'phone calls start at 6pm. The new Baha'i temple in Delhi, India—designed in the shape of a perfect lotus blossom—is officially dedicated today. Its 27 petals symbolise the one-ness of all religions.

Thursday *December 25*	Christmas Day. The Queen's Christmas message is a 10-minute film, produced by Sir David Attenborough, and beamed all over the world by satellite. The very first Royal Christmas message was made by King George V in 1932!
Friday *December 26*	Work cannot start on the new £7,000,000 Dersingham to Snettisham by-pass in Norfolk because of a rare moth 'Choristoneura lafauryana'. It would cut through Dersingham Bog, which is the moth's only known breeding site in Britain!

December

This used to be the tenth month in the old Roman calendar when the year started in March. It's also been known as the 'dead month' and the 'month of Yule'.

The Trafalgar Square Christmas Tree

The Trafalgar Square Christmas tree comes all the way from a snowy mountain near Oslo in Norway. Every year since 1947, the people of Oslo give a tree to the City of Westminster as a thank-you present for Britain's help to Norway during the 2nd World War.

Every year, the tree arrives at Felixstowe on a Friday evening, after a long journey on a low-loader and car ferry. It comes complete with a special certificate to show that there are no living creatures hiding in it. It spends the weekend at Felixstowe before making an extremely early start to arrive in Trafalgar Square in time to wake up the pigeons at 6 o'clock in the morning of Monday Dec 1.

All 20m of the tree is then decorated with 650 white lights in time for the traditional lighting-up ceremony on Thursday Dec 11. They are switched on at 6pm by His Excellency the Norwegian Ambassador, Rolf Busch, who is then thanked by the Lord Mayor of Westminster, Mrs Terence Mallinson JP.

After Christmas, on Twelfth Night, the tree will be taken down and burned in an incinerator in Richmond Park—just in case there are any spruce bark beetle eggs lurking in it!

Chit-Chat ●	The Reporter ●	Blag ★	Daily Scoop ▲
KESTRELS GET NESTING-BOXES AND CLOSED-CIRCUIT TV AT TOP OF PETERBOROUGH CATHEDRAL	FLAT EARTH SOCIETY SAYS VOYAGER'S ROUND WORLD FLIGHT IS A JOKE	PAINTING OF A STREET BY MANET FETCHES £7.7 MILLION	FOUR MILLION PEOPLE APPLY FOR BRITISH GAS SHARES

Saturday *December 27*	Helen Krasner, who set off from Brighton Pier on March 1 to walk round the coast of Britain, leaves Blaxhall near Woodbridge, Suffolk, on the last leg of her journey. So far, she's walked 7240.5km!
Sunday *December 28*	England keep the Ashes in Melbourne, Australia, defeating Australia by an innings and 14 runs.
Monday *December 29*	The Battersea Dogs' Home, London has collected 126 abandoned pets since Christmas—so far.
Tuesday *December 30*	Pelican crossings for horses are planned in Aldershot. Torrential rain and floods in Wales and northern England
Wednesday *December 31*	New Year's Eve or Hogmanay. For Sale at £690,000: the island of Great Blasket (4.827km by 0.8045km) off the west coast of Co Kerry, Ireland. New Moon—the second of the month!

Champions of 1986

Supreme Champion at Cruft's	Ginger Christmas Carol (Airedale)
Supreme Champion at Smithfield	Bruno (563kg)
Bagpipes Champion	Iain MacFadyen
Miss England	Joanne Sedgley
1986 Rose of the Year	Gentle Touch
Miss UK	Alison Slack
Miss World	Miss Trinidad and Tobago
National Snuff-Taking Champion	Gerry Anderson
Most Eatable Apple of the Year	Jonagold
Pet of the Year	Schnorbitz (14 stone St Bernard)
Junior Scrabble Champion	Richard Short
Best Station 1986	Dumfries
Miss Pears	Hannah Phillips (4)
BR Young Super Traveller of the Year	Jonathan Carter
Miss Beautiful Eyes	Angela Spencer
English Sheepdog of the Year	Cap
Smile Princess of the Year	Sally Peters
Young Engineer of the Year	Matthew Barker
Designer of the Year	Jasper Conran
Superbrain of Britain 1986	David Currah
Outstanding Young Person of the World	Dr Richard Crane
Businessman of the Year	Sir John Harvey-Jones
Pup of the Year	Viscount Grant (Afghan hound)

DUMFRIES